I0186611

Random Seed

Random Seed

Poetry

Sharon SingingMoon

Copyright © 2018 Sharon SingingMoon Feltman

All rights reserved. No part of this book may be reproduced or transmitted in any form or by any means, electronic or mechanical, or by any information or storage and retrieval system without permission in writing from the author.

All photography © Sharon SingingMoon Feltman

Compass
Flower
Press

Published by Compass Flower Press

Columbia, Missouri

ISBN: 978-1-942168-90-4

"we are singers becoming the song"......
SingingMoon

SPRING

Bird song and snow melt
hopeful signs of Spring to come
my heart leaps with joy

Spring Haiku Times Two

Wisteria pods
popping green sprouts glisten new
time to clear the beds

Equinox Moon comes
bird song is of mating calls
kitty's feeling frisky

Early Lilacs

One of those days
one of those Spring days
when my body screams
'hey, what about me'
when my head isn't quite together
when feelings transform
almost transcend phrases
demanding space on my conscious page
when rain is so right
green so green

One of those moments when
I am driven to seek a soul mate
and smell wet, early lilac blossoms
when I press my lips together
in search of another's tongue
that is not there
when the diamond between my legs
catches the light
and burns up through my belly

It's one of those days
those Spring days
and at this age of knowing
I understand these feelings
these things pass through our lives
they come and go as this rain will
though driven it now appears
knowing this, I take hold
the blazing diamond
and run joyfully
into the fiery rain

Women Squat

on prairies
behind boulders or bushes
on desert sand
mountains
as skies open to rain
women bear down
bare their valley natures
in fields
between furrows
or in stark white sterile coldness
lie legs up and open
stainless steel strangers
or grandmothers
and mothers and daughters

Women squat
knees apart bellies full and round
hands and knees
women give it all they have
their blood runs on the Mother
as She opens to their opening

Women squat
give birth in caves in canyons
in beds
in forests

Fountains flowing with life
women squat
close to the Earth
their joy in tears in tears
to bear the future
Women squat

The first sound
is a rhythmic drumming
a swooshing thump
a beating of blood flow
life pumping
to and through

it is as the ocean
and the wind
it is the heart
securing soul to body
pushing awareness
one beat at a time
into our being
connecting that being
to All

Random Seed

Spiderwort so tall and proud
along the garden path
your seductive hue draws our admiration
surrounded as you are with beauty
peony and poppy, phlox
among these purposeful plantings
still poised you stand on firm stalks
though wild you also thrive
you draw the honey bees
when sun opens your clustered blooms
to show the world your bright stamen
and yes, beside the yellow iris
you also rise in glory
but see your ill-fated sister
pushing through the driveway cracks beneath my car
I ask, "what casual wind did blow the seed
to plant you where you are?"

I stoop to pull this most persistent stunted bloom
and think
"how strange
that a simple random chance of birth
is to forever determine her diminished worth"

Just Beyond the Hills May be the Garden Un-annoyed

Today I choose the forest path, seeking brother deer
who visited my sleep
I go where few human lately walk, no trail here
except for the prints left by this nation of shy,
large-eyed creatures
Humbly I follow as their path pulls me deep into forest
freshly green with Spring
I marvel as their prints sink into rich black Earth
and seem to fly over limestone caverns
lurking just below the surface
Struggling with my own being's limitations,
unaccustomed to such flight
I determine to know deer spirit this way

Into their secret garden they pull me
never visible, yet always a rustling of leaves
and small stones just ahead
Along a dry creek bed I walk with them
their presence dancing
in the hoof-printed clay of our mighty Mother

On a small ridge between two sinking hollows
golden grasses adorn their lay-up place
Sky so vivid
the warmth so compelling
smell of sun-warmed cedar
I understand why they chose this place
I, too, rest and revel in the life I am given

Seeming to melt into the earth as red bud blossom
and bird song sensuously surround me
my senses no longer separate me
I know the unaccustomed feel of letting go mind,
of being everything
my body breath becomes a whisper

Rising up from time unnoticed
responding to what I cannot name
but trust completely
feet find the trail as deer spirit beckons me on

The trees are younger here
the limestone glows white and faintly iridescent
purple with wood violets amidst dry brown leaves
I feel rebirthing in this contrast
as above wild plum extend blossoming twigs
toward another source
they reckon with the taller young oak and sycamore
each claiming a ray or two of that necessary energy

Hoof prints of many sizes in this place
suggest a rendezvous
I imagine a dance of deer
a ceremony
perhaps too, they celebrate the coming Spring
and life
just life
Blessed Life

Sometimes it's a Song

There's beauty all around me
how the Earth astounds me
with Her surrendering and patient ways

She's the Mother Force within us
the nurturing we trust
look to Her, she'll teach you all your days

She offers us our sustenance
heals and so blesses us
shelters and provides our daily needs

Rain from the heavens
sun caressing her bosom
a fertile patch in which to plant our seed

Her blood, clean water priceless
Her bones, the stones so sacred
let Her acceptance teach us how to be

For life is more than human
four leggeds, swimmers, wingeds
from a blade of grass to an ancient tree

There's beauty all around me
how the Earth astounds me
with Her surrendering and patient ways

She's the Mother Force within us
a nurturing we trust
look to her, she'll teach you all your days

Spring

The Earth's brand new
it's a gift to me and you
we plant the seed
in the rich brown womb
rejoice in this life
we do consume

May, 2013

April 2013 Midwest drought gives way to floods...*New York Times*
February 2013 Magnitude 8 earthquake generates tsunami across pacific region, death, destruction
February 2013 Bahraini violent crack-down on protestors..... *Amnesty International*
2013 Christian cult leaders again proclaim end times, Rapture
2013 Madison, Wisconsin – 300 arrests, as capitol protest grows
2013 Tunisia – Jasmine Revolution, thousands join protest ....*BBC*
2013 California – Zimmerman acquittal sparks large protests ...*USA Today*

This is the Spring of rain here in Missouri
of rain and unexpected heat and cold
this is the Spring of abundance
the Spring for trees here in Missouri
they drink deep and flourish
their seeds shower down
sprouts claim space in my garden path
call me to bend and pull

This is the Spring of pruning, culling
cleaning out the deadwood
as Nature shows herself here in Missouri
She moves across the land with fury
taking fields and towns and children at play
reminding, reclaiming exercising her dominion

This is the Spring of rain here in Missouri
the Spring of glorious gardens
perfumed and green, wisteria, honeysuckle
rising, thriving – climbing to the stars
leaving us amazed and humbled

This is the Spring of rain here in Missouri
the Spring of unexpected heat and cold
the Spring of mighty Earth tremors
across the seas

the Goddess shakes and dances as oceans rise up
to take back what is theirs- space to ebb and flow

This is the Spring of rain here in Missouri
of rivers rising, the mighty Mississippi
doing what she does all the way to the sea
rising up, spreading out, reclaiming
reminding us of how it is
who we are
always she takes back what is hers -
space to rise and fall
renew

This is the Spring of rain here in Missouri
of rain and unexpected heat and cold
this is the Spring of warriors
workers - common folk - rising up
speaking for themselves across the globe
Egypt, Tunisia, Wisconsin, Bahrain, California
overflowing the banks of oppression
spreading out across the dessert of despair
flooding over dams, levies, armies
reminding, reclaiming what is theirs

This is the Spring of rain here in Missouri
of rain and unexpected heat and cold
this is the Spring of rapture
the Spring that was to end all
for those believers in fear and endings
deniers of life, seekers of everlasting ecstasy
prisoners of prophecy, spreading out across the land

This is the Spring of "we're still here"

To recognize, recall
this is the promised garden

This is the Spring of rain here in Missouri
rain and unexpected heat and cold
cicada hum and buzz and bug-eyed wonder
a Spring like so many Springs
filled with bird song and water and green abundance
for those who choose to notice

As we behold the daily rituals
of mating and war
of birth and death
the struggle of sprout
to reach for the sun
the dance of love
innate to each
the stone becoming sand
the rush of river to meet the sea
do we then glimpse the Sacred
know the presence of Oneness
from which our struggling mind does pull us
always within the sacred circle are we
never separate
this is the Knowing we seek

Wet Spring

If any substance understands the path of least resistance it is Water
Water finds the opportunity
and can send a torrent through

Water penetrates Earth and wood and stone
and all living beings exist in and of water

Water knows patience, too
sitting in pools in puddles in ponds
waiting until lifted up
by sacred communion with the Sun

Water knows the joy of freedom
traveling as rivulets, running to stream
to river to ocean
touching all along the way
bringing a bit of mountain to desert
dusty plain to swamp

Water gives life
Water takes life
the nest's precious egg washed from the safety of tree
the child lost in the rushing gully
the homes built where river reclaims her own
a ship at sea tossed as if a tiny toy

The sand pulled from beneath your feet
as the Moon leads a rhythmic water dance
Water
the sacred the pliant the powerful
give thanks as we curse Water
this wet Spring

There is a sense of liberation
as cold gives way to warmer
bird song
is of mating
snowdrops bloom
daffodils explore possibilities
as one brave witch hazel blossom
sends spicy drifts across the garden
they recognize the light
and respond

I am an empty bowl
formed on the wheel of the Great Mystery
in the eternal fire
alive with the ten thousand manifestations
my individual voice
is but an echo
of the vibrating universe

the elemental forces
meet on the rim
of my existence
and sing
throughout my being

Women in the Woods

We are called and we respond
rising up from our knees
from our made-up lives
we become who our secrets are
and gather in fields in woods
in circles of ceremony
in gratitude
to acknowledge
the one truth of us
through GrandMother Spirit
the fire in the center of us each
and each circle
the stones
sacred and our Earth Mother's
as we are

Our prayers
our bodies
hips called to dance
sway
as the oceans do
to the rhythm of ancient truth

we drum
sing
laugh
renew our power
as we call each singularly
all as one
with voice and silently
our fire and drum precession
alive with being
the trees open

Earth rejoices
knowing we are here
we honor Her
each other
ourselves
One body
sacred and female
the stars and GrandMother Moon
our dance
our song
our entire existence
moves to send love to the world

Upon Being

The center of your universe
is you
from within
you see and become
interact intersect intertwine

upon Being
calling forth
compelling abundance
the center of your universe
becomes positive
attracting positive
Recognizing
success and abundance
are your natural state
because you do not resist
what is yours – success
abundance
you allow the natural order

upon Being the center of your universe
joyfully accepting
what is yours
allowing positive flow
gratitude over-takes fear
your reflection lightens
draws more positive
energy radiates from your being
joy sits on your shoulder
forms a glow
as sparks fly from your fingers

upon Being
from within
the harmonious dance
draws that of love, beauty, kindness
creatively activates goodness
because you are the manifestation
of All
that is Blessed
your being
radiates positive intentions

upon Being
the center of your beauteous
bountiful universe
you draw others to the light
magnetically, magically
activating their own abundance
through the power
of Being you
give back
radiate joy, generosity
dance
meditate
on Being
the positive center
of your universe

The wren built her nest in my window box
secreted away between the impatiens and asparagus fern
up against the house seemingly safe and dry

How do I know?

Her wing brushed my cheek one afternoon
during her frantic escape
as I removed the planter box
to paint the house

Abandoned, the four tiny speckled eggs
lay cold
unchanged forever
never to take wing

Later, house painted – planter rehung
she returned to build her nest once more
in what I assume to be prime real estate

Tucked between the impatiens
and the asparagus fern
she guards the three new speckled eggs
as they lay dreaming of the sky

To Be

This is what we be
where we are
body
eyes through which to look
soul through which to see

This story
part mine
written of wordless
sounds
a life not separate
one part
of one heart

For this we praise
the force that binds
the air
the spirit
pounding in eternal rhythm
this
is what we are

Once more this pen
slides across white emptiness
in celebration and confusion
in passion and pain
again spelling questions
that unfold through the grace of their answers
turning tears to phrases
this pen, my friend
this page
reflecting truths
I hide from any other time but this
swollen darkness
creates no shadows
but this pen
outlines the shadow
my sorrow casts
the textures my joy lays
on the barren page

Struggle as I may
the captive I remain
and not reluctantly
I surrender
to this pen that beckons
a vehicle for my spirit
I and this pen
we sail across this page
to be held close makes us both
dance in the divine

Practice the Dance of Stillness

Wind communicates
Sun penetrates
The sea rises and falls
while the snowy peaks meditate
watchful
recalling
what is here now
may be lost
what is lost may be restored

When the teacher becomes fat and self-satisfied
the student becomes lazy and arrogant
as both prefer the exchange of coin
rather than that of patient practice
and insightful conversation,
all that is gained is a deepening divide
an increase in human suffering

Pork Chop Bones

While in the bathroom one morning, I heard a scratching and
banging near the window
I looked out to see a large blue jay digging up the dirt in the
window box
when I went outside to see just what that jay was up to
I found a dried out pork chop bone
strategically placed in the center
of the bare window box soil
I am not sure about the germination period for
pork chops
or even if they will thrive in a window box
but if this thing blooms
expect an invitation to a bar-b-q later this summer

Anyone with experience cultivating pork chops
in a window box, please contact me.

SUMMER

Garden meditation

Do not rush
to fill each empty space
there is no need
what is empty
has a usefulness
and will be filled in time
there is purpose in the void

Solstice

it's not the place
but the peace within
not the one who will come
but the person you are now
not the pain nor the struggle
but how you emerge
how you balance the light with the dark
act upon the knowledge gained
it could be any place
and if there is peace within
your restless spirit
has a holy refuge

Creeping Jenny
(Lysimachia Nummul Aria)

Jenny, oh sweet Jenny
you know I love you well
have I not moved stone and earth
to build this home
where forever you may dwell

Jenny, oh my Jenny
or should I not call you so
I bring sweet roses yellow
and delicate lavender sage
to set your sunny face aglow

Jenny, lovely Jenny
you are here when the Moon does rise
your gown of golden shimmers
drawing favor all around
you're like no other in my eyes

Jenny, strong-willed Jenny
tell me what is lacking in this bed
I've done all I can to keep you
here within my circle
but still you roam instead

Jenny, Creeping Jenny
this is what I love the most
no stone is rough enough
no walls can confine you
this whole garden be your host

Did you ever date a cicada
you know what I mean
they emerge
from their small dark hole
crack through their shell
a bit groggy and confused
hung-over from their time
in the damp underground
they hang about in some likely spot
evaluate the scene
maybe flit from leaf to stem
stare that bug-eyed stare
seem to wonder 'what the hell'
then, as if under a compelling spell
it all begins
the come hither hum
the Oh Baby buzz
the 'do a little dance,
make a little love, get down tonight'
of their life is on
but oh, look out
once the buzzing stops
and the deed is done
the space is littered
with the smell of sex and death

August Afternoon

breeze, hotter than the stillness it invades
pushes across the lake
throwing tiny waves against the shore
under the docks and boat house
they arrive at 4:30 – adult swim –
slowly removing their streetwear
they struggle against the years
reach out to hold each other up
trying to maintain equilibrium on the grassy slope

cotton sun hat
sensible walking shoes
lavender print cotton dress
neatly folded shoulder to shoulder, then in thirds,
is laid on the bench
beside the blue shorts, plaid shirt, flowered golfing cap
these inanimate piles of cloth have spent years
sharing benches, stools, closets
and like their owners, rest comfortably together
side by side

White lace curtains stir
sun kisses your sleeping face
tomorrow, come not
but leave us
to our sacred dance of love

Forces of Nature

first it was the wisteria
a shoot from an abandoned house
planted on the south side
where the arbor was to be
now, thee arbors later,
wisteria climbs
tendrils clinging
encircling all
the apple tree
the maple
wisteria holds tight
demands the sky be near
blooms
laughs at my containment efforts
wisteria smiles
as I whack away
trim and pinch
wisteria thrives
reaches higher in lavender glory
humming birds joyfully respond

next it was the honeysuckle
persistent relentless
creeping beneath the deck
appearing as if by magic
twining around its neighbors
taking down tomatoes
over-powering
invading fertile and fallow

rooting itself at every opportunity
not afraid to be
insistent fragrance drifting on the breeze
riding sunbeams as if
to make me smile

now it is the day lilies
glorious and bright
here today gone by night
sending out beneath the surface
that which will live on
they understand impermanence
bloom
teach us to
shine while you can
bring what you have
offer your gifts unafraid
lift your face to the sky
welcome the rain
drink it up
today is a miracle
today
this moment
is all

The storm blew in.

And he with it. Deep purple, black clouds, raging winds that unsettled dust, made leaves dance, wind chimes sing. He wore scuffed brown boots, a cowboy hat with a feathered band and tight jeans that caused women to look twice and men to check themselves. He was riding a rough red pickup, a golden retriever side-kick. On the prairie you can see it coming from a good distance, the storm clouds rolling low and dark – gathering force for their assault across the flat lands. But here in the Ozark hills, valleys, rocky ridges, deep forests can hide the truth of a coming storm 'til its right up on you – staring you in the face from across the road, from across the bar, hand up your skirt. And when the storm passes, you clean up the mud, dry things out, take stock of what was blown away and what is left behind, try to set things right again.

I scream sometimes
because Life can hurt
and cry when the sky is so blue
and fall to my knees in the grassy dew
and raise my arms in praise
and sleep a dreamless sleep
moonlight on my face
and fill the bird feeders
and pick the squash and hang the wash
and wish
and sing and dance and laugh
Life, oh Life
Beloved Life

The Tao of Kayaking
Three Treasures

Lesson from the Willow – Humility

When the river runs fast
and pushes you into the branches
don't struggle
breath, bow your head, feel the flow
re-align your boat
the river will carry you through

Message from the Eagle – Compassion

Soaring and gliding are mighty fine
but sometimes ya gotta
flap your wings hard
and gain some altitude
for a better perspective

Heron Says – Frugality

Often stillness
saving energy
while the river changes
runs on and on
is the best approach

Heat-Wave Haiku Times Two

Leaves curl as fruits drop
roots reach deep into the Earth
seeking, renewing

When hot winds push through
what is not immediate
falls away, saves strength

Susan of the Black Eyes

Is it the womb we seek
itself an ecstasy of body
swimming hole of servitude
from whence we claim our right
to blind endurance of this functional
physical apparatus
though our illusion
we are surely grieving mother
a caution filled coffin
confining us to
bones and flesh of this birth

Ay, there is this posture of preposterous communion
and this act of concealing
our inescapable mortality
in the rigorous details of keeping a time
of marking and accounting
of logic
mental exercises which we name order
refer to inconsequentially as us

Yes, we've burned the trees
who beckoned none to favor their 100 years of testifying
Yes, we've shunned their glory
shown our one half
Yes, we've dug the prairies
planned and planted
pacified ourselves with our modern piety
as if we know well more than all the whole
we are a part of

Yes, we've hunted eagle for its loyalty to mate
for its non-consideration
of our supremacy

Yes, we've chosen to kill bear
as she sleeps with her cubs
Yes, we've taken and taken
and still been left empty

Seems well we have forgotten
the salty taste
of our own sweat
and too, the sweet smell
of berry picking, row hoeing
animal talk
purple hands

Oh, too, should we take Susan of the black eye
on the rising moon
or leave her standing by the berry patch
a blessing wish
a thank you

Gasconade River

Water like silk
silence broken by laughter
we dance on the surface
kayaks skimming
while deep below
the flow of each heart's song
blends into one
trees and herons and eagles
stones and river and sky
you and I
one breath, one body

How Much the Same

Shell
fossil
burning clouds
streaked with sunlight
as if a single voice
were singing
ten thousand songs
and one song
not unlike the voices
of rain and a running stream
are dancing
the only and always dance
of dew drops
crystals
how much the same
colt skittering across a July Moon field
a bird leaving the straw womb
cracked shells
heart beat   drum chant
heart chant   drum beat
rhythm of Earth
birth rebirth
how much the same
how one and the same
you and I

Gratitude

In the early morning stillness
air cool and clean
sky not yet blue
with GrandMother Moon silver overhead
and the Sun golden
as He shows His face
above treetops to the East
there is no human sound
no voice but bird call
cricket, rippling water

I do not plan
nor promise
nor ponder possibilities
do not reflect
do not regret
but bow to the four directions
each in turn
raise my face
my arms and heart
up to the heavens
honoring Great Spirit
the Oneness of All
surrender ego for a moment
fall to my knees with gratitude
in the damp grass
whisper thank you
into the bosom of our Earth Mother

They are coming – Immigration 2018

They are coming
Those from somewhere else – the others
with their dark skin, curling hair, speaking alien tongues
their torn pockets filled with sand and clay and anguish we cannot
imagine
those from where the scars of colonization are deep, driven
through generations
deep as the blood that flows from the fingertips of children
scratching for food in the diamond mines
begging for coin as soldiers pass by in tanks that cost a lifetime of
maybes
those from where corporate exploitation steals the natural world
leaving nothing but mud and poisoned water
from where subsistence cannot beat the market place of goods
they cannot afford
of food for those above, not them
from where indigenous is trivialized, marginalized

They – the others – are not like us
they are hungry and shoeless, clothing stained with tears and sweat
risking life
they are coming in desperate waves
from plantations that were once farms growing their food
they do not understand that our need for their resources
measures more than their need for life
they are coming, running
from the civil wars we crafted
wars fueled by the weapons we supply and the lies we tell
from the horrific dictators we support
they run
from the piles of our discarded plastic and torn t-shirts given
by our feel-good faith
from the poisoned land and filthy water

54

from the once lush forests
now treeless for the grazing cattle that will become the burgers
they cannot afford to eat
from the human-made drought and famine

They are coming
running
running toward the safety that is not safe nor real for the others
those with dark skin

Should we care that they are running for their lives
running from the cartels of violence that supply our never sated
need
to escape from that which they are dying to become
they – the others - are pushing against imaginary boundaries
against real fences and future walls

They know this Earth is theirs too, not just for the pale and
wealthy
the ones born lucky of place
the ones above through no better value than random luck

They are coming from those exotic places
places where the resort walls guard against the recognition of
ourselves in their eyes
they are rushing away from pain and suffering
from torture and rape and genocide
carrying nothing but a wish, a dream
they run from increasing Earth tremors, from exploding pipelines,
exploitation
from ravaged lives
they run
from Exon Mobile and Chevron, Coca Cola and Dow Chemical
and Lockheed Martin and Monsanto and Shell and Nestle and
United Fruit and Union Carbide and Caterpillar
from the World Bank and IMF

from $1.00 a day and worker abuse
from no education no opportunity no hope for their children
they run, babies in their arms
they run to smugglers, to rafts at sea
to the river, the bridge, the tunnel entrance

They risk death
a gamble against a life of suffering
and we, lost in denial, so smugly sanctimonious in our self-proclaimed
superiority
we refuse their ships at sea
count the bodies on the shore
contemplate walls
rip babies from the breast
and build cages

Napping with Friends

cool shower
sandalwood soap
iced tea and fresh mint
poetry and a guitar
in the four poster bed
while the ceiling fan spins
kisses in secret places
turn our separate imperfections
into a perfect string of pearls

Micky's Purple Bike

Its summer and I'm off on my bike
in the cool morning breeze
I hear birds singing
in the maple trees

I may zip past the post office
or stop by the mill
or coast to the school house
and pedal hard up the hill

Then round the stop sign, turn right
and down the hill I fly
to the cottonwood tree
I wave to neighbors as I speed by

I stop at the old safe and the general store
just say, hello, maybe get a pop
then off to the big barn
so much to do, I just can't stop

I whiz through the air, wind in my face
I lean in on the fast curves
I feel free, I feel brave
I pedal strong with muscle and nerve

it's something I like
this power I give my purple bike

AUTUMN

Autumn's Treasure

one yellow rose blooms
season's last daisy stands proud
breathe in, live, dream now

From Spiral

The wild things know
change in the wind
sun setting earlier
rotation shifting
the wild things feel season after season
rebirthing
they chase their tails
around persimmon trees and eat so much
rain makes nuts plentiful
they fall for us
the wild things know
to gather the bounty
pad the den
prepare for migration
they know, the wild things
to soak up this Autumn sun heat
they know
the ones that are wild
those not afraid of their instincts
the wild things who are still aware
of stars, water, wind
they read these signs with one eye
they know
the wild things
their young are weaned
their stores are hidden
their fur grows thick

Ordinary, mostly unnoticed, she was however a woman of strong appetites, driven by patterns set in childhood, like a trail through deepest wood, tread upon step by step, worn down to bedrock.

She found herself to be in a place, a time that, like so many places and times, valued women made of clay thrown on the wheels of men and shaped as willed by others. Even so, coming to know

herself as more than a vessel holding the fantasies of others, she broke free, formed and re-formed her own destiny with tools she found along the trail and those things she could steal.

Witch hazel glows golden
crimson flames of the burning bush
shimmy and shiver
with a chill wind
that whispers and whistles
of seasons to come
green has gone
yellow carpets what was
as we let go that
and embrace this here and now

Otherness

There is no other
just the One
we are born of Earth of Air and Water
it is the strangeness of mind
that nurtures fear and separateness
that blinds the heart
consumes compassion
builds the walls
that create the myth of other

Night does not blame the dawn
for stealing her stars' glorious light

Nor does the Sun in his radiance
forget the Earth
but warms her with golden caresses

The silver Moon does not struggle
as she sweeps across the heavens
in her divine dance

The sea has no fear as it rushes to sand and stone
knowing its sweet salty kisses
will not be refused

The soaring bird does not doubt the invisible current
that lifts him up
but floats wings spread believing

The seed, though hidden in deep and holy darkness
performs the ancient ritual of creation and re-creation
because there be nothing else

What more is there to know?

Forgiveness begins with you
forgive yourself for every choice
you ever made
that you would not make today
celebrate yourself
for knowing now
what you did not know then
and dance beloveds dance

Autumn Grace

Lone cricket croons
seductive indigo sky
promises forgotten
kept
tangles of green
tipped in Autumn dress
I let go Summer
glorious as you are
I open welcome
await with joy
the change
swirling sensuous dance
of burning reds yellows
burgundies ablaze
coming darkness
renewal rebirth
the seed beneath
dark rich soil
digging in resting
patient

Fire speaks
one language
dances with steps
tuned to wind rhythm
ancient
without words
one soul
bends
toward Earth
stretches
to sky
we know
beyond this being and time
there is comfort
in the One Truth

There are days
when our souls cry out
for meaning
and trees are so beautiful
we almost cry
when the blue sky caresses us
and all seems well
and there are days
when we carry our sad computers
into the Geek Squad for emergency treatment
biting our nails
as all the photos
and poems and fragments of ourselves
may disappear

Oh, Beloveds
you must not think there is no rhyme
no reason

You can see the Mystery unfold
feel the sacred kiss here, now

Know that you are your own truth
no excuses no doubts

Sure as this river flows rolls on
and this rock rotates
spinning spinning

Oh Beloveds
So must you spin and spin
on this rock and roll on
your rhyme
your reason
your rhythm
is the truth of you

Beloveds
Rock this rock with your presence
gently

Spinning spinning
Rock this rock and roll gently on

you must not think there is no rhyme
no reason

You can see the Mystery unfold

Sky is gray
over blue
I wish for you
your obsession with rain
when you come again
thunder will rush
from the lightening

We've known this land
this sky
air we breathe has been breath
forever
we know these hills
though their ways have been abandoned
we've known this land
before the trees were gone
and stones were dug
and ground to powder
to be formed, reformed
to human demands
we've known this place
as well as suckling knows their
Mother's breast
and as that breast has swollen and subsided
so this vexation and rage
as we see so much
of what we've known
be changed so fast
we remember this hill
with trees
now plagued
with the human tumors
of our imagination
yes, we've loved this land
this home and heart
of us
we've set our minds and bodies to rejoicing
on this ridge
in times past and hope to with the winds of the future
we've lost our hearts
on this slope
as oaks, uprooted

cried and screamed
and no one else could hear
but us
we've known these mammals
reptiles
insects, some unseen
some seen fleeing
from the falling
and burning
of their own habitation
we've seen and known
this creek
this blood of our own Earth Mother
flowing
now clogged
with old boots
bread wrappers
bottles
we have loved this place
though now it reeks
with oil smells and machine noise
and our own indecision

The Poet

His pen flies, ink flows, spelling
spewing verse in talismanic script
pretentious ordination
a façade, known yet denied

His page curling, yellowed,
holds fleeting visions yet incomplete
or unattained
at sixty and two thirds

At his desk, reflections of a greying sky
and naked trees
press against the pane
he stares through dry, dying potted life

dusty on the sill
still struggling against neglect
Oh, for a phrase without redundancy
the joy of all once new

the return of love once traded for just sex
Again he reaches for the glass – extension
of the bottle -
imprinted by oily fingers

caressed by crusty lips
A sacred chalice, broiling cauldron
Doorway to the wordly world that bears down hard
bares his loins to careless winds

ripping fragile branches from his imagination
shattering contrivances
Leaving now only raw
tasteless greasy smudges

Meditation I

waves wash over me
mind energy
oceans of fear
doubt, judgments, plans
do not hold these thoughts
be as the sand upon the beach
receiving the rushing tide
releasing
though moved by this rushing
as sand and pebble are pushed
pulled
remain present in the now
unattached to the constant waves
of mind energy

Meditation II: Judgment

go inside
find peace
is peace a judgment
longing brings discontent
why suffer?
we cannot avoid it
language – judgment
extracting one object
one feeling one thought
from the whole
naming creates judgment
boundaries
you....me....them....us
we suffer because we name ourselves
as separate
we do unto others
because we name them "other"

Meditation III

Dark and light
arise of the same source
joy and sorrow
are equal sides of one root
war and peace
aspects of one nature
the essence of being
is above, below
before and following
know the center
of the center
this knowing
will set you free

Meditation IV

stop
breathe, touch something
fully engage with the experience
notice how Earth feels
against your skin
the texture of water
sun caressing
your body is a blessing
a source
practice
just be with sensation now
notice joy as you breathe deeply
this is the way to the center

Meditation V: Times Four Haiku

Do not fear your life
to recognize your feelings
your hands heart and mind

Is to accept life
vulnerability, yes
but a blessing, too

Investigate self
mind energy claims, controls
only if we choose

Don't identify
with constant jibber-jabber
seek center stillness

WINTER

The Promise of Winter Solstice

Ice crystals glisten
on dry grass as soft winds pass
the light be restored

Easy
coffee
toast and apple butter
Then came the winter
hiding just outside
seeping quietly
through cracks
under doors

I did not recognize
or did not acknowledge
the coming cold
as it made known the weak places
allowing the sunshine to be
even more than before

From Some Other Time

Along the trail by the bluffs
river wind in my face
hands freeze
to hold this poem to a page
sky gray water
watery gray sky
only the silhouette of trees and the line of land
where each becomes individual
the question comes again
from within
the answer
in the river flowing so
even as a mighty wind
pushes on against the persistent
and inevitable
this path
the one the sleeping trees take
holds my step to it
as I struggle for my place
the Great Mystery
holds the place of me
for times when I have no recognition
yet, to the woods I shall return
rhythms dancing
drum beats of my Being
hum of my heart
are sounds I've come to trust

When Love Is Gone

Your hands nervously place
and replace themselves
you pour the wine
your voice
the laugh
I feel I know
we speak of incidentals
your eyes move
here
there
don't look at me
please look at me

We dine as per appointment
we hurry
more than we can
stand
we do not touch
and on the street
again
safe
we leave each other
your lips
brush mine
in the evening light
silver
sliver of the Moon
alone in the early night sky

Crystal Trees

The frozen night cradles us
in its silence
our steps and creaking branches
heavy with ice
are the only sounds
this darkness cloaks
the day's crystal trees
and brilliant sky
and holds fast the ice to our hearts
this life
we leave our mark
as we move
one to the next

Why is there not a Poem
in these evening shadowed rooms
quiet, left-over
party paper
singing from the ceiling
running over ashtrays
abandoned glasses
half-full of some watery fantasies
in the silken folds of the gown
I've worn since early last night
in its pockets
stuffed with call-me-tomorrows
on the leaves of the jade plant
looking from my desk
to the dirty snow below
silent trees
frosty branches
they have a song
but why is there not a poem
in the bathtub
full of once hot water
waiting obediently
where I left it
in the needles
full of girlish rushes
on the canvas
in the journal
in this cloudy frustration
chilling
empty feeling
on the slushy sidewalk
where I freeze my face
to find a word to say
why is there not a poem

Live each moment with intention
live as if you are alive
trust your being
is a precious gift
and that you bring meaning
to us all

For Cortney

old friends bring news
share their life with you
give and trust
want to know
don't need to hear your whole story
pick up where you left off
know who you are, were
have already forgiven you
remember that night, that time
think your dance is a good dance
have wiped your tears, held your hand
shared moments and memories
can assume they are welcome
and they always are
old friends believe you truly care
and you do
they want to listen, hear you
have no need to fear
trust your concern
laugh with you
at you – know it's OK
embrace your uniqueness
as you treasure theirs

And just like that, there it was. Predicted, yet unexpected. Why now? Today? An inconvenience, so denied. Wrong turn down a dead-end. His luck, which he had always regarded as exceptionalism, may have run out.

He had been warned, discussed, and then dismissed the signs. Fires devouring forests, fields, homes and people. Parched plains, fish kills, sweeping droughts, torrential rains, frequent quakes, eruptions. All just fodder for alarmists.

He had barely noticed as the blue of the sky turned greenish-grey day after day or that the stars of his childhood had disappeared, maybe months ago, beneath blankets of poisonous smog.

How long since he'd seen those ancient trees along the coastal highway? He seemed to recall something about lumber and trade wars, but really, the details eluded him and the story faded from his newsfeed.

He, being so busy, was only marginally aware of the fleeing masses, dismissing them as greedy, needy, poor and brown, who came to steal, to rape and replace. Their stories added no value to his importance.

And when that soft greenish-grey sky cracked open, let loose with a fury, gullies becoming rivers, becoming lakes, becoming a filthy brown sea of floating human waste as far as he could see, he ran.

He told himself he would be OK. It was not his home floating amidst trucks and trees, dead animals; not his granny left in the house where he had spent summers swinging on a tire swing... he had put away such childish things.

Though he did not believe, he was one who hedged his bets, covered his bases, just in case. The gates, the guards, the hidden stores, underground fantasies of safety. He congratulated himself, money well spent, money piled high —

salvation purchased...........he had no idea what was coming

Oh, Missouri

Oh, Missouri, how often I have tried to travel on
Second Mother, my Missouri
Feels like this is just where I belong

I headed for the desert
when the cactus were in bloom
found I missed the lilacs and their sweet Spring perfume

Oh, Missouri, how often I have tried to travel on
second Mother, my Missouri
feels like this might be where I belong

Took off for the mountains
and their sprawling pines
but I yearned to see the Ozarks' painted hills
in Autumn time

Oh, Missouri, how often I have tried to travel on
second Mother, my Missouri
feels like this might be where I belong

Slipped out to the ocean
to lie on a sandy beach
missed the stoned water singing of Splice Creek

Oh, Missouri, how often I have tried to travel on
second Mother, my Missouri
feels like this might be where I belong

Rich in life and at the center
of a poet's soul
all the wonders that you are
may I come to know

Oh, Missouri, how often I have tried to travel on
second Mother, my Missouri
guess the Spirit knows where I belong

The Fire Speaks of Love

Dry pine needles
dry leaves
burn fast
flame up and are gone
little heat
lots of smoke when damp

Deadwood soft
catches on slower
but the heart is soft and weak
smokes
has little substance
to sustain a burn
creates ash
leaves no coals to stir up later

Twigs
if you arrange them right
will give some flame
and if they're not too dead
too green
can burn to start a larger branch

It's the hard wood, though, that can sustain a burn
if you can get the kindling going
hot enough to catch a flame
split it so the heart is exposed
get it good and hot
should go all night
and leave some coals
to stir into a flame
next morning

In the dark

In the dark alone
I do not mourn
for what is not fills the air with what is
a drifting lullaby
while clouds snuggle in to caress the trees
starlight is a faint illuminated truth
as one wonders upon inevitabilities
in the dark alone
oh do not mourn
for what is not
leaves room for what is
a sweet simple taste
of the eternal now
Oh the ringing consternation
is as imagined
as the lines from star to star
in our mind's constellations
for the dark is alone
and does not mourn
for what is not
shakes the sky with what is
our dreams up and walking
the steps are burning
burning like the stars' existence
fuels itself
with our flaming darkness
do not mourn
you're never alone
for this life is not all there is

Moon of Desire

I want it to be a poem
as the wind and soft clouds
touch Her
so I want to be touched

I want it
to be a poem
softly curled
around my body
warm and moist
as the clouds touch Her

I want it to be
a poem
silver light shimmering
transforming
the dark of solitude
to bright new fullness

Like Her
I want it to be a poem
glowing radiant
on the black sheets
of night
disappearing
into newness

I want it to be
a poem
meaningful

as irresistible
as the force
driving my red blood, sir
like Her

I want it to be
a poem
flowing on
page upon page
night after night
dry grass
ablaze
green sprouts
like Her

I want it to be a poem
rising cool and white
fire reflection
lingering on
past dawn
like Her

I want it to be a poem

In this land of men calling from towers for others to fall to their knees.........

What name, the Goddess

Do not ask...you know deep within

She is every woman
back to the beginning
full breasted, fertile
honored on cave walls
even further, deeper
rising from the Sacred loom

She is the soil, the stone
the flowing spring
melting snow
raging river
the heat exploding mountains
the turquoise sea
rich and salty and alive

She is the woman gave you life
the Mother
to whom you shall return
She be, Blessed Be
that part of your own being
that calls you once again
to love
to nurture
to refrain
when anger demands
commands your heart and hands

She is every name
you have ever uttered
in passion   in pain

in joy in prayer
and a name so ancient
too sacred to speak

She is the face of your own
Mother Sister
Lover Daughter

She is the stillness the life force
the dance of Spirit
Unique Singular
Universal
do not make Her less

for She allows you to be
without demanding you bend your knee
to Her
you are the flower of the field
the flow of the stream
the breeze that whispers
you are Her breath
Her heartbeat
no more
no less

That which has been hidden or denied

For Donna

In the deep and holy darkness
damp fertile
filled with possibilities
All that may be
forms shape
acquires substance
takes root
gains awareness
fills itself with being
as our own breath
lifts our breast

In the deep and holy darkness
dwell all that may be
feeding
becoming

All that is hidden or denied
the seed of life
of hope
of prayer or despair
resides as a tender sprout beneath the surface
in dark struggle
with eyes closed
arms outstretched
reaching for the light

In the deep and holy darkness
demands are made
of faith
of intention and tenacity
all that may be
exists in sacred balance
rich and ready
with potential
and may burst forth or shrivel
becoming sustenance

For the deep and holy darkness
does not judge
does not chose
is just is

In the deep and holy darkness
doubt not
the formed and formless
thought and deed
ethereal and material
will reach the light
will return
to the deep and holy darkness

As the light is born
of darkness
so too are we cradled
in the tender and fertile darkness

The word that can
be written
will not express it
the sound
that can be shaped
will but repeat it
the eye that can see it
looks within
the heart that can hear it
beats eternal

To touch it
be very still
to see it
close your eyes
to be there
go no where

Estate Sale

The line curves down the front walk past
well-maintained borders and neatly trimmed lawn,
past parked cars blocking half the street,
past annoyed neighbors.
Anxious purchasers queued up the block
and around the corner imagine bargain bounty
while curious lookers tightly clutch paper coffee cups as they
gauge the size of the house hopefully
excitedly plotting their nosing about. A stranger's home
has become a market stall
their life's accumulated treasures on display.
Glassware, shining on the dining set,
only $1,400 – such a steal
carpets and clothing, sofas and chairs
the bed they slept in for so long.
Among the tools and trinkets
portraits of the grandkids wait in the garage
for love and appreciation from those
who did not know them.
The moments and minutes and meanings of a life
heartbeats, breaths, hours and days
were traded for the stuff now stacked on tables
tags dangling, prices flexible, half off on Sunday
picked through and haggled over by strangers,
to be scattered here and there.
Next week, they say, the house will be for sale.

When death is stalking
breathing breathless at my nape

And I am worn renouncing
all the faith I promised to grasp

As untold poetry forgets the page
and I mourn the loss of inspired rage

When dull wits savor celestial auras
and loves soft petals return to their origins

As flocks unforgotten by seasonal transitions
feather the spaces into submission

As the Moon pulsates, rolling the distant sea
reminding rhythms, so ancient a dance 'twill be

That I to this Earth will give back what is me

When you are ready to hear
you will hear
for the music is in the wind and the sand
the sage and the cedar

the Medicine is in you

When you are ready to sing
you will sing
for the song is the air that we breathe
and the Earth Mother's love
and the beat of your blood

the Medicine is in you

When you are ready to beat the drum
the rhythm will come
as the sound of your steps
on the path of your life
as the roaring in your ears

the Medicine is in you

When you are ready to dance
you will remember the dance
as the dance you've been dancing
for lifetimes uncounted
and dreams manifested
and lessons begat of those dreams

the Medicine is in you

When you are ready to dance

you will remember the dance
as the dance you've been dancing
for lifetimes uncounted
and dreams manifested
and lessons begat of those dreams

the Medicine is in you

the Medicine is in you

the Medicine is in you

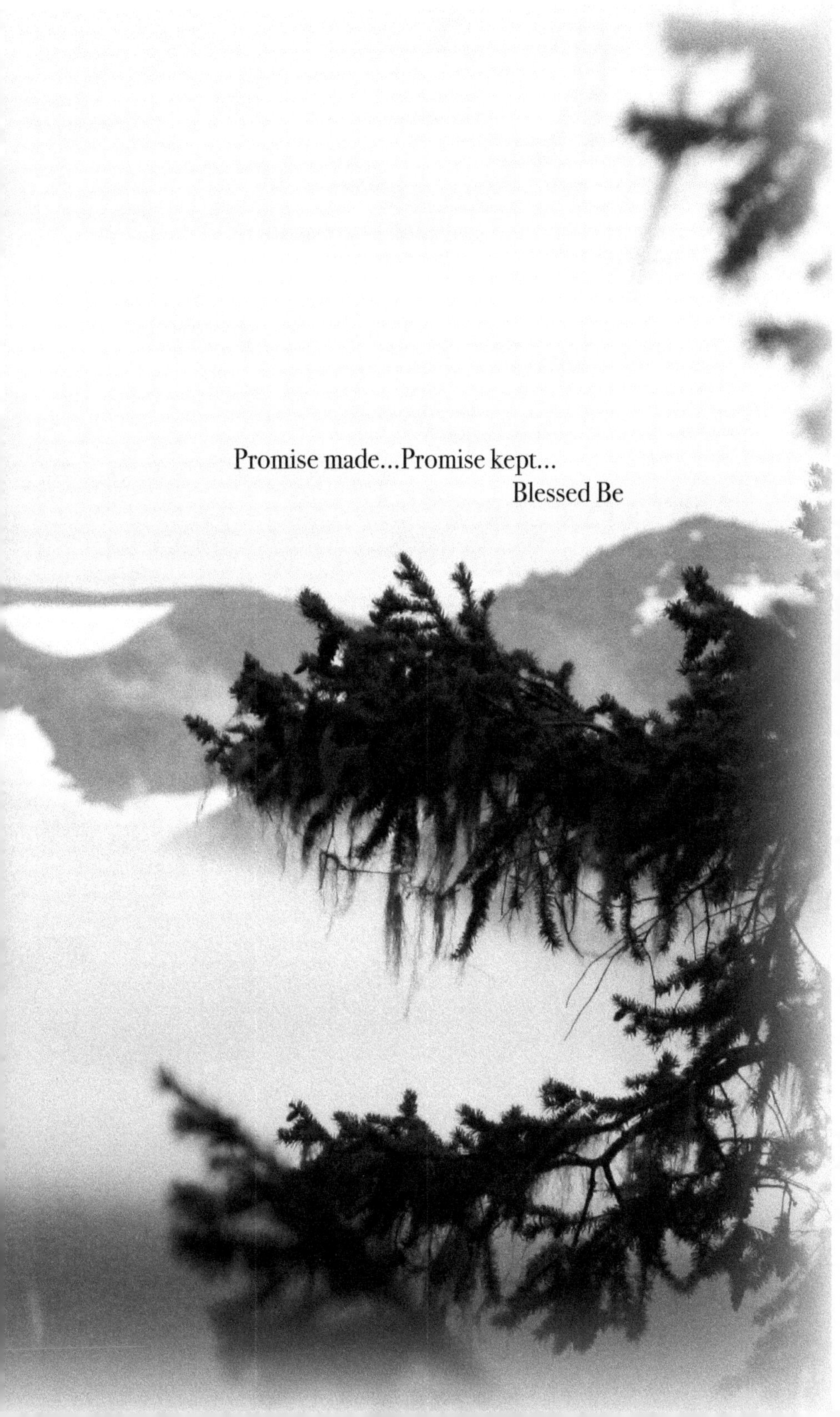

Promise made…Promise kept…
Blessed Be

www.ingramcontent.com/pod-product-compliance
Lightning Source LLC
Chambersburg PA
CBHW071231090426
42736CB00014B/3045

What experts are saying about *A Tale of Two Husbands*

"*A Tale of Two Husbands* is a charming story that gives a clear picture of married life and the path to making it successful and happy."

"*A stirling page turner!* This book is wonderful allegory that provides insightful advice to benefit any marriage."

Shazeen Qamar, MS
Clinical Psychologist, Professional Therapist and Counselor.

———

"While reading *A Tale of Two Husbands*, I was astonished by how much the strategies recommended in this book resemble my own advice to clients. It shows women how to calmly and peacefully approach their husbands to get the results they want and the love they need."

"The lessons in *this book will make your marriage heaven on earth.*"

Ninda Samer
Professional Relationship Expert and Life Coach

"I enjoyed the story. It is a compelling read. And I believe wise. There are some universal truths in it and a lot to be said for the book's approach."

Carolyn Doyle
Registered Clinical Social Worker, Psychotherapist

———

"When true love meets the practicalities of domestic life, it can quickly lose its shine and become a confusing tangle of disappointments. What I love about Chris and Angela's engaging and profoundly useful story is its magic formula—a handful of simple questions that will help transform a frustrating marriage into a real partnership. Highly recommended."

"This book is a delightful little gift to the world—just the right amount of simple, practical insights and tools to help create domestic harmony."

Graeme Barry, B.Sc., ACC
ICF Associate Certified Coach

"The beauty of this book lies in its simplicity. It guides the reader through an easy, step-by-step communication process that will help any woman get what she wants from her marriage."

"A Tale of Two Husbands is a wonderful book—a must read for any woman intent on improving her relationship."

Enitame Tejiri, B.Sc.
Relationship Counsellor and Writer

—

"Just when you thought all hope was lost, these writers beautifully explain how couples can save their marriages and spend a satisfying life together."

Ayesha Asghar
Clinical Psychologist